LOVE

peter max©

EDITORIAL ASSISTANCE BY ARJUNA (VICTOR ZURBEL)

THIS BOOK IS DEDICATED TO
MY BELOVED PARENTS, MY WIFE — NITHYA (LIZ),
MY SON — PRABU (ADAM COSMO),
MY DAUGHTER — JOYTHI (LIBRA ASTRO)

WILLIAM MORROW AND COMPANY, INC.
NEW YORK • 1970

Love is the immediate
way to Truth
or the Kingdom of God.

It is the principle of
creation and the highest
expression of the
soul-force.

Love is the
law of life.
To love is to
fulfill the law.
And to fulfill the law
means
eternal peace and
everlasting
happiness.

It was the driving force behind
Moses, Jesus,
Buddha, Krishna,
Mohammed, St. Francis,
and all the great
sages and
saints.

It is the magic wand
in the hand
of the devotee by
which he
conquers the entire
world.

Man is one. God is one. Love is one.
We are all the fruits of one tree
and the leaves of one branch.
Everyone is God in the process
of evolution.
Identify yourself with everything
that lives.
Love all God's creation.
Love even the leaf;
love the animals, love the plants,
love everything.
Feel that the one power
of God works through all hands,
sees through all eyes,
hears through all ears.

There is no virtue higher than love;
there is no treasure higher than love;
there is no knowledge higher
than love;
there is no religion higher than love;
there is no truth higher than love.
My dear children of love, tread the
path of love. This is your highest
duty. You have taken this body
to achieve love,
which alone is the goal
of life.

Live in love.

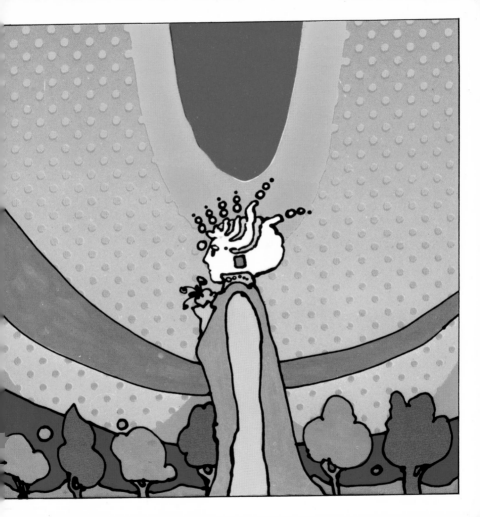

Breathe in love.

Meditate in love.

Move in love.

Sing in love.

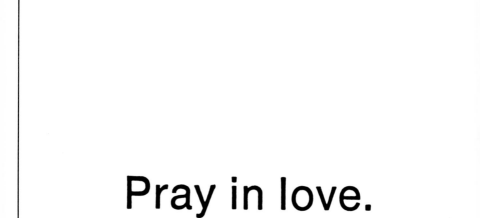

Pray in love.

Die in love.

Purify your thoughts, speech
and actions in the fire
of love.

Bathe and plunge in
the sacred ocean of love.

Imbibe the honey
of love and become an
embodiment of love.

Spread the message of love.
Let the spirtual message of
oneness
and the divine call to unity,
friendship, and amicable
cooperation
reach the hearts of all
and awaken love and brotherhood
in the bosom of humanity.
Let all the world be
circled with love.